Home Baking Business

Caren Curb

Every effort has been made to track the quotations back to their original sources. If errors have mistakenly occurred, corrections will be made in subsequent editions.

CadArm Publications
Casa Grande, Arizona 85122
Copyright © 2014 Gerald Shingleton

ISBN: 10: 1496192699
ISBN-13: 9781496192691

Table Of Contents

Introduction

I want to thank and congratulate you for choosing
the book, *"Home Baking Business"*. Keep in mind,
however, this is a continuation or 2nd book in a
series. The first explains the real beginnings of a
home baking for profit endeavor without explaining
the business aspects. It is strongly suggested that
you read *"Home Baking for Profit"* before tackling
this subject.

Caren Curb never imagined her cookie recipes
would be so popular in town. Businesses started
hounding her for more variety. They began
suggesting that she open her own shop. Well the
popularity naturally grew into something she didn't
expect. Before too long, she worked on a marketing
plan, got a food handler certificate, business
license, and home occupation permit. Now she's in

a position to grow with employees and finding out the sky is the limit. There's all kinds of opportunities for anyone who has a home kitchen, opening stores on Etsy and other craft or home business marketing storefronts, and selling at local fairs, festivals, and farmers markets. There's also grocery stores, food service businesses and other shops. Basically, Caren explains the ***business*** steps to take, after all, success begins with the first steps as she explained in her first book in this series. There's even a few "winning" recipes that will get you started. Once your cookies are in the public, you'll be able to build a reputation and go from there. Then it's time to face the dreaded business legitimization. This book covers all that.

1 CASE HISTORY

Home baking for profit is a cottage industry. There are other money making opportunities too. Topics for consideration includes many producers, all working from their homes, and usually part time. For example, some workers typically engage in tasks such as sewing, crafts, internet sales, lace-making, wall hangings or household manufacturing. But to start making money right-a-way, I recommend **home baking**.

Just to give you a little background, working from home is catching on. A century ago, that's the way things were, generally. But more and more regulations, zoning laws, and just *pain-in-the-ass* complexities caused a shift in commerce. It used to be that some industries, which were usually operated from large centralized factories, engaged small cottage industries, but that was before the Industrial Revolution. Business operators would travel around, buying raw materials, delivering them to people who would work on them, and then collected the finished goods to sell, or typically to ship to another market.

The Industrial Revolution redirected things which really began in Western Europe and that slowed down the popular cottage businesses. At that time, the big business people had the ability to expand the scale of their operations. Still, cottage industries remained in a different niche since a large proportion of the population engaged in agriculture. The farmers and their families, who often had both the time and the desire to earn additional income during the part of the year (winter), when there was little work to do farming, would sell produce by the farm's roadside.

So now here we are today. The use of the term has expanded and used in legal terminology. Governing authorities now recognize the particular necessity of supplemental income. Laws are currently designed to accommodate this need and the word is used to refer to any event which allows a large number of people to work part time, usually from home.

For example, *eBay* is said to have spawned a cottage industry of people who buy surplus merchandise, and sell it on their auction system. Another example of a cottage industry is the *"ecosystem of devoted news sites"* dedicated to the prediction of products that *Apple Inc.* will roll out next. The list goes on and on.

A home baking business is unique because it is the easiest and least expensive way to make money. I'm not talking about a whole lot of money to start. But you never know what can happen in this business. My first book in this series explained how "testing the waters" is the best approach to begin your quest, usually as a fun charitable fund raising activity. But when success is eminent, it is time to prepare for growth.

There are hundreds of stories. My favorite is one that Marlo Thomas wrote years ago about such an enterprise. She claimed that Kathleen King was the *Queen of Cookies* by the time she was 11. She grew up on a farm, where hard work was just natural and expected. One day her big sister announced she wanted to take a job in town; one that offered more opportunities to meet boys.

That's when Kathleen took over the duties of baking cookies for the family's roadside stand. Everyone loved the idea that a kid was selling cookies, so they'd ask if they could buy some, then she'd run back inside and bring out a warm bag. Looking back at the beginning of this successful business venture, she recalled that her parents bought the ingredients, she got the eggs from the farm, and so everything she made was 100 percent profit.

It got to the point that she was selling so many cookies, after a while, her father renegotiated a deal! He naturally wanted in on the action. By the time Kathleen turned 21, she and her father were full time partners and were ready to put successful baking skills to an even bigger test. They took her cookies to the street -- a location just seven miles from the family farm, but in the center of the bustling resort community of South Hampton, New York -- just hours from Manhattan.

After she graduated from college, her mother noticed there was a bakery for rent. Two other bakeries had failed in that spot, so people said it was a terrible location; but she was convinced she could make it work. She figured they just didn't have the right ingredients. So she spent the winter testing recipes and opened Kathleen's Bake Shop with $5,000 that she saved from selling cookies on the farm and produce stands in the area. She told friends and family that there was always time to start a new dream. You can tell this story started out about a young entrepreneur who eventually ended up with a wildly successful cookie business. But there's a catch.

The problem was her business sense. She had none and eventually relied heavily on a couple of business consultants who were dishonest and skimmed profits for themselves. The results were devastating. She fought back though and rebuilt her business. She's now in her 40's with an enterprise worth 16 million dollars.

This true story is meant to show that you can do anything. Keep in mind that enthusiasm and drive are more important than the obstacles that you will need to address and resolve. But with the following guidance, most concerns, advice, and questions will be addressed and answered.

2 WHY BE LEGITAMATE?

Most people decide to launch their foray into the world of small business ownership because they have an exceptional product. Perhaps friends have chanted infinite praises of your pies, or everyone who tries your cookies believes baking is your destiny. Although it takes a great service and a solid business plan to be successful, your product is the first thing to think about.

You probably began your small enterprise strictly as a hobby. You love to cook. Selling your product started out as a fund-raising activity for your local service club. But the *goodies* are getting more and more popular and expansion is encouraged. The next step seems scary. After all, no one complained about purchasing your product to help out the local Rotary Club. Heck, even the Girl Scouts were caught selling their products in front of the Marijuana Dispensary. That made the news but no official damnation, after all.

So why complicate things by getting involved with legitimizing the practice? Well, the answer to this very important question depends on where you see this going. Do you want to Limit yourself, constrain your talents to mediocrity, inhibit growth, and just plain operate on the fringe? You reason that if someone complains about the venture, you'll just fold up and shut it down.

But, there's a whole other perspective to think about. If your product is great and in demand, you could follow a different path; a way to capitalize and invite *easy street* to come into your life. Have you considered this?

1. A legitimate and prosperous business enterprise could eventually be marketed and sold for a profit. Don't think otherwise. After all, when you can show tax returns with a profit, it is definitely worth an investment for someone. Name and goodwill is worth something!

2. **Franchise.** Provide training to others who wish to enjoy profits from a part time home business. Share success recipes. Charge a business set-up fee and enjoy royalty payments. Imagine what can be done inside this arena of ideas. It could very well mean paid traveling expenses and a profit to boot.

3. **Hire** assistants to make business life a little easier. Think about what this would mean, not just for yourself, but for any young person anxious to get work experience. Minimum wage jobs are getting more and more scarce, but if your home occupation permit allows one or two

employees, that could be a wonderful opportunity. Or, at the very least, what about giving those grandchildren some responsible positions?

4. **Consulting services.** Train beginners and set up shop in their own homes. Guide them into setting up a legal enterprise. Then, purchase their products for wholesale and make money selling retail. This can even work in reverse.

5. **Sell** your home products to retail stores and food-service facilities.

6. **Marketing.** Being legit means more avenues are opened up like chamber of commerce, internet sales, etc.

There is, of course, a downside like paying sales tax, income tax, business license fees, food handler card, inspections, insurance, and paperwork, to name a few. In my first book, twenty percent of sales went to a local charity. The next step regains that loss but is used for other expenses. Your charitable efforts will probably suffer as a result, but the sky is the limit when it comes to future expansion possibilities. And as the profits bloom, so can your charitable contributions!

3 BECOME A REAL BUSINESS

Legality of home-based bakeries in your area.

While opening a home-based confectionary might seem easy, you should be aware that there can be limitations. For example, in some jurisdictions, home-based food preparations may be prohibited. In others, there are many permit and insurance requirements that you'll have to meet before opening your home-bakery's doors. Check with your country or state's health department or food and agriculture agency to determine if starting a home-based food preparation business is legal. If worse comes to worse, consider relocating. I would!

If I were to consider the best cottage food law, it would encompasses a number of features which would first include the ability to make an unlimited income. The whole point of going into business is to make money. So if there's a law that restricts how much can be made, use your imagination on how franchising and consultants can become part of your particular enterprise. Keep in mind that you want to provide your family with a good source of income and give them the things they need to live a healthy and meaningful life. As a sidebar in this effort, think how others will benefit and help the economy, provide superior goods and services to members of your community and even participate in the "greening" of America (if you are into that).

But when the day ends and all is said and done, as any wise business owner knows, you absolutely want to make money! So the question to be asked and answered is, "Which jurisdiction and state has the best cottage food law?" The answer is simple, any cottage food state that allows you to process the food product you want to sell, from your home kitchen, with limited rules and regulations, allowing you to prepare, non-hazardous food products that can be sold in the manner of your choosing, and allowing you to make as much revenue as possible. Naturally, you also want to support and maintain a lifestyle that provides your family with all their needs. So let's take a look at some of the various authorities. Like I said, you may be inclined to entertain a move, if your current location is *bad for business*.

Cottage Industry Laws

Before embarking on your cottage industry enterprise, you should observe your country or state's cottage industry laws. Not all jurisdictions have such laws, and if they do they can vary considerably. Examples of favorable laws are Arizona, Colorado, Florida and

Illinois. California passed a pretty decent law in early 2014 too. Some states such as Alabama and Kentucky have very strict cottage industry laws, while others have pending laws. If you live where there are no cottage laws, such as Alaska, Montana or Delaware, you will have to rent a kitchen and sell your products at farmer's markets.

After you've determined that you can open a home-based bakery, you'll want to modify your home kitchen. In other words, turn it into a decent commercial food preparation area. This will allow you to sell baked goods to customers. I say this since there's a good chance that you'll have to modify your kitchen somewhat before inspectors will certify your kitchen. Research what modifications you have to make and complete them before an inspector makes his first visit. You could be lucky though, in my case, there's no inspection required by the health department though they publish guidelines on their website.

But I personally find this advice very useful in my own situation. I designed a rather unique center-island equipped with four elevated clean 5 gallon buckets to store flour, sugar, brown sugar, and oatmeal. The counter surface is smooth, non-porous *Corian* whish is sanitary, and easily cleaned. I turned a large coat closet into a separate pantry to keep all business related items and food supplies away from other domestic goods.

Licenses, Permits and Zoning

To have your home kitchen approved as a cottage industry kitchen, be prepared to have it inspected by some governing authority, whether that is a zoning department, department of agriculture, a department of health, or some combination of these. In some areas, where there are cottage industry laws, the state Legislature in particular, prohibits local health departments from regulating cottage businesses. Instead, enforcement is by *both* state and local health departments who keep records of complaints about cottage industry foods.

To be able to sell food products to the public, your cottage industry business can only sell foods that are not potentially hazardous. Food types range widely, and may include cakes, certain pies, popcorn, candy, jams and jellies. Prepared foods that are not shelf-stable are not allowed. The idea is that an intended consumer can be protected by cottage industry laws.

Generally, laws allow sales only to individuals and not on a wholesale basis, although this is not always the case. Online selling and out-of-state selling will generally be prohibited and some jurisdictions only allow for selling at farmer's markets or bake sales.

Packaging and Labeling

As a cottage industry food purveyor, you may be

required to package and label your products in a particular way. Your governing authority may ask you to list all food ingredients in descending order of use as well as provide contact information such as the address where the product was baked, and if legally required, indicate on the label that the food item was prepared in an uninspected or unlicensed kitchen.

I use the Avery labels (1 inch by 2 5/8 inch, number 5160) and can get all the info required by the enforcing health agency.

Examples of Favorable Authorities

North Carolina has one of the most progressive cottage food laws in the nation; not only allowing its citizens to make a variety of non-hazardous food products but also providing workshops that assist in product development, business operations, marketing, social media tactics and more. The state makes it clear they are **"pro"** food entrepreneur, even showcasing vendors the opportunity to displaying and marketing their products in the NC "General Store" and the annual *Eat NC Got to be Festival* every spring.

Another state, Arizona, has a favorable cottage food law. There are no revenue limitations, the state website is relatively easy to navigate, there's an informative video that actually promotes the cottage food industry and they also allow "group homes" to operate *home-based* bakeries with specific requirements. This is an added bonus since many developmentally disabled adults find it next to impossible to find employment. Okay now what?

Food Preparation

If you're serious about expansion, starting and building an artisan food business, and your jurisdiction does not allow a domestic kitchen, you'll need to find a commercial kitchen space in which to bake. Before you take that step however, you may be able to continue operating under your state's cottage food laws. There are exceptions to the rules and you'll need to look into it.

For example, currently 31 states in the U.S. have what are called "Cottage Food Laws" which allow you to use your own kitchen to produce food products; baked goods, candy, canned jams or jellies, dry mixes, spices and sauces. Of course you must still adhere to the FDA's good manufacturing practices, but beyond that, the rules and regulations vary from state to state and even within states, among cities, counties and towns. Since this is a very serious aspect of your business, common sense is extremely important and it's also a good idea to check with the appropriate agency to get the most up-to-date information for your circumstances.

Some states allow you to produce food in your home kitchen. Many states don't want you to take that chance either and you will not qualify to work under

Cottage Food Laws if you have any pets in the house. Some states, such as North Carolina, Ohio and Oregon, require the Department of Agriculture to inspect a food processor's home. Other states, including Texas, Arkansas and Indiana, don't require an inspection. Presumably they don't mind a dog hair or two in the fruit butter.

In my own personal situation, among family, I am known for keeping my kitchen clean as I work. I clean up as I go because it bothers me to have a mess everywhere. That said, it's still unlikely I would take the chance of baking in an unsanitary condition, especially since I have two cats. I'm careful to lock them in a separate room when in production and scrub down the entire kitchen. Though it's never happened when I bake at home for pleasure, I personally would never have wanted the chance of a cat hair to show up in a cookie.

The laws and regulations apply not just to the actual kitchen facilities. They also specify where and how you can sell products, how the foodstuffs must be packaged and labeled and limit the gross income from sales. In Virginia for example, a cottage food production operation may sell its foods only directly to an individual consumer for his own consumption and not for resale or use in commercial food preparation. The food sales of the cottage food production operation takes place only at the operator's home or at a farmers market. A cottage food production operation is not allowed to sell its foods by mail order or through the

Internet. Annual gross income is limited to $50,000 and products must include a label that identifies the name and address of the food production operation and the statement *"NOT FOR RESALE – PROCESSED AND PREPARED WITHOUT STATE INSPECTION."*

In other states, such as Florida and Michigan, laws are similar, although the annual gross revenue limit is $15,000. In Texas, cottage food producers can ONLY sell from their homes and not at farmer's markets. Arizona allows home baked goods to be sold via retail stores as long as you have a food handler card, are registered with the state's Home Baked and Confectionery Goods Program and your product is appropriately labeled.

One thing that seems to be consistent across the board is that none of the Cottage food laws specify where and how you can sell products. You might say that states allow cottage food producers to sell online. However, I've heard a lot of discussion about internet sales along with accusations that not everyone is playing fairly by this part of the laws. Some people may very well be getting away with it. Karma will catch up to them – what else can you say?

On the other hand, maybe some accusers are misinterpreting the mandate. To be clear, not being allowed to SELL online does not mean you can't have a web site, blog, Facebook page, Twitter account or any other online presence. You can. But, you are NOT permitted to set up a shopping cart on your or any other web site and allow people purchase. All exchanges of money must take place in face to face transactions.

Personally, I find the cost of shipping too much to maintain profitability. Product arrival will always take time away from freshness and could even be stale by the time of sampling. I would not recommend it.

However, my cookies are in such high demand that I'll send a complimentary batch to friends, relatives, and even servicemen from my hometown. They absolutely love and crave these home-feel care packages.

4 STEPS TO SUCCESS

Well now it's time to promote your product. If you discover that door to door selling is not your cup-of-tea, consider local consignment outlets or farmers market alternatives. Arizona, for example, has a wonderful home baking outlet called the *Blue Myrtle House*. A destination establishment like this will promote your business, though it won't be promoting your product specifically. Vending spaces are also typically available in just about any downtown area too.

One of the easiest and cheapest ways to stimulate sales is by using Facebook. The cool thing about Facebook is you can tell all your friends and family about your product, and then have them tell all their friends and family about your product and so on.

There are two ways you can do this. The easiest is to just use your personal Facebook page. Another way is to create a Fan page on Facebook that is all about your product. Google and look up the *Blue Myrtle House* fan page to give you an idea how it works. To create your own fan page you must have your own personal page. If you don't have a Facebook page, sign up for one. Then go to the appropriate link to create a fan page.

I do not recommend heading to the bank, but starting really small instead. Let your business finance itself, believe me, using a credit card and having a huge loan on your shoulders is a heavy burden to carry. It takes a lot of the fun out of business ownership.

So before doing all the paper work, concentrate on setting up proper marketing and business development plans. One great marketing strategy is to tweet your treats. I'm talking about Twitter. By opening a Twitter account you can alert people interested in your product. You may also google ideas like the following. http://www.bluemyrtlehouse.com/cottagelaw.html#sth ash.skC8NO3r.dpuf

Photograph your cookies to use in your marketing materials, such as portfolios, brochures and ads. Send a news release to local media outlets about your new business. Take samples of your cookies to local stores, cafes and caterers, and ask about offering your cookies as part of their service. Not that I agree, but If you want to ship your cookies, consider selling them through a website.

A business plan is an essential roadmap for business success. This living document generally projects 3-5 years ahead and outlines the route to take to grow revenues.

Now if your dream is a part time business for a small

support income, there's no chance of thinking big. But still keep some future strategies in the back of your mind. If your delicious munchies grow in demand, you'll have to start thinking beyond the box. There's something called *putting-out system* which, in the industry, is a means of subcontracting work. Historically it was also known as the *workshop system* and the *domestic system*. You probably will have to have workshops to train prospective consultants, if this be the case.

Putting-out is a clever way to leverage. Work is contracted by you, as a central agent to subcontractors who complete the work in off-site facilities, either in their own homes or in facilities with multiple bakers. Historically, this type of domestic system was suited to the old days because workers did not have to travel from home to work which was quite impracticable, due to the lack of adequate roads and footpaths. Members of the household spent many hours in farm or household tasks. Early factory owners sometimes had to build dormitories to house workers, especially girls and women. *Putting-out* workers had some flexibility to balance farm and household chores with the *putting-out* work, this being especially important in winter.

Well now, let's get our tasks in order.

Step 1 (Food Handler Card or Certificate)

Google *Food Handler Card* for your state or country.

Eventually, you'll land on the internet site that instructs you what is necessary for your home bakery business. Most likely, there will be a training and testing exam. Don't worry, you are guaranteed to pass, but you are required to watch online videos and then take a short multiple choice exam (well, that's what I had to do).

The fee varies for a card or certificate but it is not at all expensive (maybe $10). What you will learn is proper hand washing, FDA Food Codes, Federal Food Safety, and a lot about transmitted disease. Temperature controls, cooking temperatures, reheating, proper thawing, and cleaning will also be addressed.

The occupational licensing board that regulates food sales teaches the laws regarding food businesses operated from home. Remember, some states may require you to have a separate kitchen with its own oven, refrigerator and other equipment. Other states only require that your kitchen tools and food ingredients be separate from your personal ones. A health department official may need to inspect your home business kitchen. Apply for other food permits as required.

Step 2 (Make your Business Official)

1. Obtain a business license from your city or county government office. What is required varies but most likely you'll be required to get finger-printed at the local crime enforcement facility. A recent 2 x 2 color photo

will be needed for filing as well.

2. Apply and obtain a Home Occupation Permit from the jurisdiction planning department. Zoning laws generally prohibit other uses in a residential district but when there's no added traffic, advertising, or business customers, the permit allows minor business activity.

3. Contact your state's comptrollers or taxation office about a sales tax permit if sales tax is collected on food in your state.

4. If your business name will be different from your given name, file a *doing-business-as* statement with your county.

5. Open a checking-savings account in the business name. Use the account specifically for business expenses. That makes keeping track of income and expenses a lot easier for tax filing purposes.

6. At some point, I would hire a draftsman to prepare an "as-built" floor plan of your home. The scaled drawing will be very useful. Outline the area used in your business (kitchen, dining table, pantry, and office desk area). The total area of your house and the total area of business use will be used in calculating the home-office deductions you are entitled to when filing income taxes.

There's a technical difficulty that needs mentioning here. In fact, almost everyone who uses a home office deduction is probably in violation of federal standards and they don't even know it. The federal ADA-Americans with Disability Act requires "accessible" features whenever there are employees or business guests to your home office. By definition, a home office deduction means that you utilize the area for customers. I probably only have one customer a year, but that would qualify the space for a deduction. The problem is, access to the premises is in violation because the step is more than one-half inch above the entry stoop (okay – give me a break!). I do not have an accessible toilet either, but I do have handles instead of knob door hardware (good for arthritic hands).

6. Purchase business insurance to cover your home business. If you're running a business from your home, you may not have enough insurance to protect your business equipment. A typical homeowners policy provides only $2,500 coverage for business equipment, which is usually not enough to cover all of your business property. You may also need coverage for liability and lost income. Insurance companies differ considerably in the types of business operations they will cover under the various options they offer. So it's wise to shop around for coverage options as well as price.

Note: Regardless of the type of policy you choose, if you're a professional working out of your home, you probably need professional liability insurance. Some types of in-home businesses, such as those that make or sell food products or sell home-made personal care products, may have to buy special policies.

To insure your business, you have three basic choices, depending on the nature of your business and the insurance company you buy it from. It would be best to personally discuss these options with your insurance broker, but essentially they are...

1. Homeowners Policy Endorsement

You may be able to add a simple endorsement to your existing homeowners policy to double your standard coverage for business equipment such as computers. For as little as $25 you can raise the policy limits from $2,500 to $5,000. Some insurance companies will allow you to increase your coverage up to $10,000 in increments of $2,500. You can also buy a homeowners liability endorsement. You need liability coverage in case clients or delivery people get hurt on your premises. They may trip and fall down your front steps, for example, and sue you for failure to keep the steps in a safe condition.

The homeowners liability endorsement is typically available only to businesses that have few business-related visitors, such as writers. But some insurers will provide this kind of endorsement to piano teachers, for example, depending on the number of students. These endorsements are available in most states.

2. In-Home Business Policy/Program

An in-home business policy provides more comprehensive coverage for business equipment and liability than a homeowners policy endorsement. These policies, which may also be called in-home business endorsements, vary significantly depending on the insurer.

In addition to protection for your business property, most policies reimburse you for the loss of important papers and records, accounts receivable and off-site business property. Some will pay for the income you lose (business interruption) in the event your home is so badly damaged by a fire or other disaster that it can't be used for a while. They'll also pay for the extra expense of operating out of a temporary location.

Some in-home business policies allow a certain number of full-time employees, generally up to three.

In-home business policies generally include broader liability insurance for higher amounts of coverage. They may offer protection against lawsuits for injuries caused by the products or services you offer, for example.

In-home business policies are available from homeowners insurance companies and specialty insurers that sell stand-alone in-home business policies. This means that you don't have to purchase your homeowners insurance from them.

3. Business owners Policy (BOP)

Created specifically for small-to-mid-size businesses, this policy is an excellent solution if your home-based business operates in more than one location. A BOP, like the in-home business policy, covers business property and equipment, loss of income, extra expense and liability. However, the coverage is on a much broader scale than the in-home business policy.

A BOP doesn't include workers compensation, health or disability insurance. If you have employees, you'll need separate policies.

Automobile Coverage Insurance

If you are using your car for business activities -- transporting supplies or products or visiting customers -- you need to make certain that your automobile insurance will protect you from accidents that may occur while you're on business. Contact your home or auto insurer.

Step 3 (Business Overhead and Operation)

Decide what types of cookies you will be baking. You can specialize in one type of cookie, such as chocolate chip or shaped and decorated sugar cookies, or you can offer a variety. If you will be the sole baker, consider the amount of time you have vs. the amount of time each type of cookie takes to create. Drop cookies take less time than decorated ones. Also think about storage and delivery. Decorated cookies will require special storage and delivery to prevent them from being ruined. Create a price for each type of cookie by single purchase and in bulk. Your prices need to include the cost of ingredients, preparation time, business overhead and your desired profit margin.

Purchase the equipment and supplies need to create your cookies. These items include bowls, utensils, mixers, baking pans and measuring devises, which need to be kept separate from your personal cooking items. Buy packaging materials, such as plastic wrap or bags, and pastry boxes to store and deliver your cookies. If your state requires food labels, use computer label stickers to print your labels and stick to the cookie packaging.

Step 4 (Marketing and Selling)

Find commercial kitchen space

Many people begin by baking from their home kitchens, but once they want to think about selling them for retail, their home kitchen usually doesn't cut it. Hence, many home bakers opt to move their baking operation to a certified commercial kitchen space they can rent by the hour, such as a commissary kitchen. Retirement communities usually have kitchens in their recreation buildings too. Churches also may be able to accommodate you with a generous donation. This is usually a more realistic option than purchasing a commercial bakery outright.

Operating a Bakery

Cottage industry confectioneries can offer consumers a

cozy home-baked alternative to mass-produced or industrialized facilities with their assortment of homemade and handcrafted cakes and cookies. However, in order for such places to legally operate in certain jurisdictions, they must abide by the local industry regulations and laws. Depending on where you choose to establish your bakery, some areas have more latitude than others. In the alternative, of course, mail order and personal delivery services is a way to keep overhead costs down.

Create a Strong and Unique Product

Your product should offer something special in order to draw customers. Perhaps you offer the only place in the neighborhood or sell delicious treats door to door. Your product may end up the talk of the town like a mouth-watering cinnamon roll or a cultural and traditional cream-cheese treat. There could be a niche to fulfill a demand for gluten-free cakes. Keep in mind though, if you want to open a cupcake shop, and your town already has five of them, you many struggle to differentiate yourself.

Think about achieving profitability

When creating your baked goods, you want to make sure you are offering a product that can hold its own. If you plan to use the finest spices and real butter in your recipes, for instance, you need to make sure you will make enough on each sale to afford the ingredients and the time it takes to bake it, while still bringing in a profit.

Keep great taste a priority

People need food to survive, but most people want their food to taste good. This is especially true for baked goods. It's likely that your product already makes taste buds sing, or you would not be thinking about making a career of baking. Just be sure this is the case for a better chance at success in your endeavor.

Prepare for Business Ownership

Before you consider expanding your hobby to own a successful bakery business, be sure you understand what is involved with owning your own operation. From the costs and responsibilities, think critically about what it means.

Understand the financial obligations

Be sure you consider the costs involved in starting a new business. Starting a bakery business usually requires fees for certified kitchen space, large-volume production equipment, bulk ingredients and required fees for business licenses and food handler's certifications, depending on your state requirements. To cover these costs, you may require a small business loan and investors.

Prepare for the time commitment

If you have a family, another job, or other personal commitments, be sure to take a serious look at how starting your own business will affect these parts of your life.

Write a business plan

Preparing a business plan is critical to any start-up business. Without clear goals and a path to follow, starting your own business can leave you feeling lost and under-prepared. Learn how to write a business plan before launching into your new career.

If you tested the waters, as I showed you how in my first book in this series, the ultimate success and failures of where your business is headed becomes quite clear. Determine what variety of products work. In other words, feedback from customers determines what needs to be improved upon or even eliminated.

Once settled, decide how the growth can be handled. In other words, assistance from outside sources can spread the duties, speed up the process, and allow for better productivity. Growth may lead to bigger and better outcomes, but be very careful and analytical.

Learn more about how to start a restaurant

Food service industry businesses will fail if there's not a complete understanding what it is all about. Don't even entertain the idea without professional assistance. A financial package will include leasing a space, building or improving a tenant space, and properly designing the facility to operate well and meet all accessible and health related regulations.

Procure the proper equipment and supplies. Your trusty countertop mixer might have worked wonders for all of your small batch recipes, but once you are whipping up cakes, tarts and pies for the masses, you will need the right commercial equipment and supplies to accommodate the workload. This includes everything from pots and pans to ovens, refrigeration, pan racks and display cases.

Be Open to Alternatives

Your passion for baking is commendable. Opening a home bakery is a fine goal, but it certainly isn't for everyone. If your dream to open your own bakery business does not seem like it will pan out, there are other options and these alternatives may be more to your liking.

Consider operating a franchise

Many home bakers find that they are more drawn to investing in a franchise than starting a business totally from scratch, since the product, the concept and the processes have been tried and proven. Investing in a bakery franchise may restrict your creativity or hamper your individual product, but it can provide a great path for success if small business ownership is your ultimate goal.

Take over an existing bakery

You may have grown your home bakery business to the point where expansion is eminent. Taking over an existing bakery can be a good way to get your shoe in the door at a place that has already been established, reducing some of the headache of finding a space and buying all new equipment. Beware of buying a place if the reputation may be tarnished, or if you have doubts about the location, because these are things that are difficult and sometimes impossible to change, even under new ownership.

Keep it a hobby (the alternative)

Starting a bakery operation from your home can be a good move if you have all the requisite pieces in place for a successful operation. Many people find that their home bakery business provides them with a way to do what they love while also making a profit. Again, as a reminder, be sure to investigate local laws before fully investing in a new business, but know that there is usually a way to make it work if you have the skill, the financial support and the drive to make it happen.

After investigating all your options and all the requirements for starting a bakery business from home, you may realize that a home bakery is simply not in your future. There is no shame in continuing to bake as a hobby for your friends and family. Chances are that your talents and treats will brighten a day here and there, which will keep you driven and dedicated even if you do have to keep your day job.

5 THE SKY'S THE LIMIT

To give you an idea of what potential lies ahead, a successful bakery man told his story in a magazine interview a few years back. He bought a house that had a separate commercial kitchen on the ground floor. The upper floor was the residence living space, kind of a mixed-use arrangement. Because he used the profits from selling his other home, he was able to buy the place and be debt free. That meant he made a profit from the very first order. He didn't want it to be big at first, just something to do because he lost his job and was bored.

But it grew despite efforts to keep it small. The gross revenue turned out to be $1700.00 for one day. Word of mouth popularity grew into wholesale, corporate, national, and individual clients in just under two years of operation. Now he has to turn down business.

He claimed to have owned three startup businesses in his life, one of those being a marketing company. But before he started this new venture, he had to re-learn the tools that work on the web. The point is, that with the right preparation, the sky is the limit on income.

Currently he has outgrown a huge 1200 sf bakery and equipment. He had to buy more pans, stagger oven space, outgrew three big KA mixers, and had to add more work stations. He needed a fourth oven and a commercial mixer. He never thought he'd need them.

Business plans are to open a small retail bakery in a nearby target city, but all baking will be from his current location. He wants to continue building a clientele before paying rent somewhere. He has all the fixtures, decorations, displays, and equipment for the bakery already purchased, again debt free. He claims to always be a careful planner and never to stop studying business issues, baking practices, and the market.

His commercial kitchen took two years to plan and build. He didn't just jump in and wing it. The public face of a business is important if you want to make serious money.

In your case, I hope you get to realize your dream. No matter how big you get, schedule things around your personal schedule. This would be great to keep your personal life in order while making money.

OTHER BOOKS BY THE AUTHOR

The first book in this series will personally help you get over the hurdle of starting out with absolutely no experience whatsoever. Go to

http://www.amazon.com/Home-Baking-Profit-Building-Business/dp/1496123301/ref=sr_1_1?ie=UTF8&qid=1394399053&sr=8-1&keywords=caren+curb